SPEAK UP I CAN'T HEAR YOU®

THE VOICE OF A WOMAN

DR. NEISA R. JENKINS,
EdD, RHIA, FAHIMA

MCCLURE PUBLISHING, INC.

Copyright © 2023

Dr. Neisa Jenkins for McClure Publishing, Inc.

All rights reserved. Printed and bound in the United States of America. According to the 1976 United States Copyright Act, no part of this book may be reproduced or utilized in any form or by any means, electronic or mechanical, including photocopying, recording, or by any information storage or retrieval system, except by a reviewer who may quote brief passages in a review to be printed in a magazine or newspaper, without permission in writing from the Publisher: Inquiries should be addressed to McClure Publishing, Inc. Permissions Department, 398 West Army Trail Road, Bloomingdale, IL 60108. First Printing: November 11, 2023.

ISBN-13: 979-8-9877802-4-4

Scriptures marked KJV are taken from the KING JAMES VERSION (KJV): KING JAMES VERSION, public domain.

Amplified Bible (AMP) Copyright © 1954, 1958, 1962, 1964, 1965, 1987 by The Lockman Foundation, La Habra, CA. All rights reserved. Used by Permission.

Scriptures marked NIV are taken from the NEW INTERNATIONAL VERSION (NIV): Scripture taken from THE HOLY BIBLE, NEW INTERNATIONAL VERSION®. Copyright© 1973, 1978, 1984, 2011 by Biblica, Inc.™. Used by permission of Zondervan.

To order additional copies, please contact:

McClure Publishing, Inc.
https://McClurePublishing.com
800.659.4908

Dr. Neisa Jenkins
www.iambeautifultooministry.org

This book is dedicated to my daughter, Kamara Jenkins, my eternal business partner. I am a better individual because of you. I love you and Charlie forever.

~ and ~

To all those who feel they do not have a voice. Your voice is meant to be heard and your dreams, visions and aspirations can manifest all over the world.

Table of Contents

                                                                       Page

INTRODUCTION

The Night Prior to the Interview 13

The Day at the Studio 21

My Voice, My Purpose 43

It's All Worth Talking About If It Helps Someone Else: Communicating 49

The Voice Of A Woman 59

Always Infuse Love When You Speak 65

MY VOICE 71

BIOGRAPHY

JOURNAL

INTRODUCTION

Within the pages of this book, you will discover the interview about Speak Up I Can't Hear You®, along with personal stories about life intertwined. As the interview is taking place, I reflect on experiences that are relevant to the interview. As you read what I have written, you too may find areas in your life where you were stifled and couldn't move forward because you did not speak up.

Every day of our lives we are presented with opportunities to speak up and share our thoughts about the things we see, hear and experience. Somewhere along the way we choose to say, "I am not going to say anything," or we say, "I am going to keep my opinion to myself." Oftentimes we convince ourselves that our opinion doesn't matter. We even convince ourselves that we should keep our dreams and visions to ourselves.

We have to change our thought pattern, knowing that we may help someone who is going through a similar situation, and they just need to hear what we have to say.

I don't know how many times I shared something personal while standing in front of a microphone, or in a small group of women, or during a phone call, and someone will call, email, text, or come up to me and say thank you for sharing your experience with us. I thought I was the only one who went through that situation.

One important fact I have learned, and I carry it with me every day of my life, our experiences are not just for us. They are for someone else who needs our help. When we share something with one or two people, they share it with others and so on. Our voice has the potential to change the world and that is so powerful and so meaningful.

Women are born with an instinct like no other. We know when something is not right. We have a heightened awareness.

I remember when my daughter was sick, I had no idea she was going to die. I woke up at about 2:00 AM after sitting with her at the hospital one day. I came home to take a shower and get some sleep, but at 2:00 AM, I woke up and I said, "I must get to the hospital, Kami needs to know I am there, and I need to see her."

I was with her when she took her last breath. What if I hadn't gone to the hospital when I did. What if I hadn't followed my motherly instinct. I had the privilege of being with her when she was born and when she died.

Within me is a sound echoing of wisdom. It is bursting at the seams. Speaking publicly is what I am able to do now that I have gotten passed what others think or might say. Do I still get a little anxiety along with butterflies in my stomach, I certainly do but the call is so much bigger than me. I have a message that will benefit so many people; therefore, I must speak up so that others can hear my voice and receive the knowledge and wisdom that I must share. It is detrimental to my success to instruct, encourage, and strengthen those who are listening. The benefit will be a two-edged encounter.

When we have something to say and we don't say it, the words get trapped inside of us. We may allow others to say whatever they want without us giving our opinion. There was a time when I had to learn not to have an opinion about some things. Although, there is a saying that everyone is entitled to their own opinion. What we have to say is important and vital to our growth and the expansion of others. I have found that we have expectations for people, and they have no idea because we don't share what our expectations are.

This book includes pages for journaling, with questions and statements that can help you reflect on your life and identify areas where you can grow. Use these prompts to fill in your thoughts and ideas.

If you encounter a question or statement that you cannot think of the answer, you can move on to the next one and return to it later. Write in a space that allows your thoughts to flow freely.

SPEAK UP, I CAN'T HEAR YOU®
THE VOICE OF A WOMAN

The Night Prior to the Interview

The night before the interview, I was sitting in my home office going through my notes. I wanted to be sure that I would not miss any information that would be vital to the viewers/listeners. This interview had the potential to be heard on one of the top shows in the country, so only my best will do. Rehearsing over and over again helps me stay on track, although, there are times I speak off the cuff. You know what I mean, you get lost in your thoughts and your mind veers off on to another thought without any warning.

After reviewing my notes, I decided to wine-down on my sofa while listening to my thoughts surrounded by my favorite scent Bryce Canyon candle by Balmori Balmori. It was very peaceful. In the silence, I could hear rain softly hitting my windows. Sometimes I just sit on the porch and listen to the rain. The sound stills me as I think about how much we need the rain physically, mentally, and spiritually. It offers us a time of cleansing.

Before going into my kitchen to get a cup of chamomile tea so that I can be sure to have a restful night's sleep, my phone rings.

"Hello."

"Hey, its Jim."

"Oh! This is a surprise. Are we still on for tomorrow?"

"Yes, I was just calling to see if you had any more questions regarding the show."

"I know what I am going to wear but are there any colors I should keep in mind?"

"Well, I am wearing a gray suit, a dark gray tie with purple and beige stripes."

Speak Up, I Can't Hear You®
The Voice of a Woman

"That's great because my dress is pink."

"Marvelous."

"Just relax you will do well, so don't be nervous."

"I have done this several times and each time, I am always a little nervous."

"No, worries. Our editor will edit the show before it airs."

"Glad to hear. Well, I am fine. Looking forward to this interview because it has been a long time coming. I need to get my message out there."

"Well, glad I reached out. I will see you tomorrow."

"Okay, I will be there an hour before the taping."

"Enjoy your night."

"You too."

I remember being young and hotheaded. I would get angry quickly, I think it was just something I learned from my Mother. It wasn't good or bad. It just was something in us that wouldn't allow us to talk long, before you knew it, we were ready to fight. We went from zero to a hundred in the blink of an eye. This behavior was contrary to God's word in James 1:19, "Let every man be swift to hear, slow to speak, slow to anger." As time went on, I would ask myself what are you so angry about? What happened to you that made you so angry? I think it was just unaddressed behavior that kept people at bay, they didn't mess with you and if they did, they would have a force to reckon with. It is not something that I am proud of, and I must admit, I have learned to control my temper.

I try to think things through and think about the consequences. I don't think that part of me is totally gone. God has humbled me over the years, and he has done it in ways that are irreversible. The irony of it is, my Mother was instrumental in the humbling process. She and I had a conversation once, I don't remember how old I was, I just remember her saying, "You've got to change your attitude." Now we had this conversation several times. Lol, it wasn't really a conversation as much as it was her lecturing me.

There was one particular afternoon my Mom and I were in the kitchen at our home on Armory Place, and something happened. She said, "You've got to change your attitude," something changed inside of me at that moment.

Over a period of time, I took a deep look inside myself and I learned that my anger wasn't working for me it was working against me and all the promises and purpose that was inside of me. I realized that there was a better way. I no longer wanted to be angry about nothing or something. What I do know is that I was spoiled and used to getting what I wanted, and that behavior seemed appropriate in doing so. The truth is it was selfish behavior that kept me from dealing with the truth of each situation.

I remember getting so angry when I was a child that I walked in my room slammed the door and threw something at the window over my bed and it shattered into pieces. On another occasion, I remember getting so mad at my sister about something so silly I can't even remember the context, but I didn't speak to her for months. Oh, not to mention the precious time that was lost laughing and learning together during that period of our lives. There have been many other occasions where my temper got the best of me. I am still a work in progress, but I try to think things through and ask questions that lead to a resolution.

The next morning while I was driving to the studio, I was speaking in my car the answers to the prerequisite questions that I was given. My expression is as if I am in front of the audience. I bet people in the other cars are wondering *what is she doing*. It is strange how we always think about or assume what others are thinking.

SPEAK UP, I CAN'T HEAR YOU®
THE VOICE OF A WOMAN

The Day at the Studio

I pulled up to the studio in downtown Atlanta on Peachtree Street in my black Cadillac CT6 3.0L. I remember I was listening to "Lord, Do It For Me" by Zacardi Cortez. This song reminds me that I don't always know what I need but God does.

The valet driver ran over to my car door to park my car. As I was going through the revolving door, I see someone I know leaving. I waved but continued walking toward the security desk to sign in.

"I'm Dr. Neisa Jenkins here to see Mr. Jim Fogle."

The security guard said, "Yes. Mr. Fogle is expecting you. I need to see your ID."

"Great. Thank you." As I handed the guard my driver's license.

He looked at my license and then looked at me. While handing me my license back, he said, "Take the elevator to the seventh floor then go to Suite 1300."

Arriving on the seventh floor, I started walking in the wrong direction and had to turn back in the direction of Suite 1300. As I opened the door, the receptionist said, "Hello, you must be Dr. Jenkins."

"Yes," smiling.

"Mr. Fogle is expecting you. Someone will come and bring you to the studio."

"I'll take a seat. Thanks."

Browsing the nice artwork on the walls, one captured my attention. A red stallion suited for riding going in the direction of a sunset in an open field of green grass. Then the door opened.

"Hi, I am Bryce here to take you to Mr. Fogle's office. How are you today?"

"I am well and you?"

Speak Up, I Can't Hear You®
The Voice of a Woman

"It really turned out to be a nice day today after that peaceful rain we had last night."

"Correct. My thoughts exactly."

Walking down a long corridor on castle color hardwood flooring, I noticed the pictures of Jim and entertainers nicely organized on the walls. The flooring is what I have in my kitchen. This is why I noticed it.

Bryce opened the door to the studio to let me in first then he said, "Let me take you directly to Mr. Fogle's office. He will go over some things with you before going to the set."

Mr. Fogle stood behind his desk and said, "Welcome to Jim Fogle Studios. It is so nice to have you join us today. Would you like coffee, water, or juice?"

"I'll take cranberry juice if you have any."

"Sure, Bryce can you get Dr. Jenkins juice from the frig?

"Have a seat. I want to go over a few preliminaries with you before we go next door to the studio."

Bryce heads over to the frig to get the juice in Mr. Fogle's office frig while taking a glass off the bar. He sits both in front of Dr. Jenkins on Mr. Fogle's coasters on his desk.

"Thanks Bryce. I appreciate it."

After Bryce leaves the office, Mr. Fogle makes mention of how nice it is to work with people that are willing to work.

"So, you met Laurie my receptionist?

"Isn't she beautiful? She comes in with designer clothes, and I am not sure how she does it on the salary that I am paying her."

I laughed because nowadays people have two to three jobs and maybe another one on the side.

SPEAK UP, I CAN'T HEAR YOU®
THE VOICE OF A WOMAN

After going over the preliminaries, we are finally headed to the studio. I am already getting excited about sharing the theme, "Speak Up, I Can't Hear You.®" This message came to me during a time that I felt like my voice was stifled and needed to tell my story.

Jim walks me over to an All-Modern Miller chair. The interview is taking place on a platform type stage with a nice backdrop that has a huge screen to the side of the back wall with large lettering, JIM FOGLE SHOW. Between us is a round coffee table from RH with two coffee mugs that has the same lettering as the backdrop.

Today is a special day for me, I decided to wear my Kendra dress by Tracy Nicole, a well-known designer in Atlanta. This dress is a power dress, it commands the attention of the room but holds its femininity in its blush pink color. I had to wear my pearl earrings and matching pearl necklace that Mr. Jerry gave me.

He is a close friend who I met a few years ago. We talk about life and the goodness of God all the time.

The audience, camera men, and director are already in place waiting for me and Jim. Intro music starts playing and the lights go up. Now, I am really feeling this is going to happen.

Jim sits down in his chair and introduces me after he opens the show. The energy in this place is electrifying.

"I'm your host, Jim Fogle. I have with me Dr. Neisa Jenkins."

"Hello everyone. I am here to talk about my book SPEAK UP, I CAN'T HEAR YOU - The Voice of a Woman."

"What would your target audience discover reading this book?"

Speak Up, I Can't Hear You®
The Voice of a Woman

"My target audience will discover how to use their voice and feel comfortable using their voice to let people know their thoughts, their opinions, their visions, their dreams, to share any of their ideas with others.

"A lot of times as women we get so bogged down in family stuff and we don't think that people really want to hear what we have to say because we are the person who fixes everything for everybody else. But we don't really get to tell our own stories. We don't get to talk about what things are particularly important to us in our lives, like our dreams, our goals, and our visions. And so, I think we have to encourage each other as women in order to get people to feel comfortable speaking up, to take a platform and share their thoughts. And it doesn't matter how big or how small the topic or issue is. It is plainly important that women speak out about issues and build up and strengthen one another." Dr. Jenkins explained.

"Wow, which sounds fascinating, Dr. Neisa. And why are you qualified to write this book?"

"I'm qualified to write this book. Not only have I lived this actual experience myself, but in my second education after obtaining my doctoral degree, I have been able to present around the United States and share my thoughts and ideas with women, conduct various research, provide documentation to prove that research, and share those thoughts and ideas with women. I have experienced bringing women together in forums several times over the last few years qualifies me to speak on this issue. Especially, as I hear from other women who have struggles with things like not only women related issues, but they struggle with things in regard to their families, their children, the workplace, career choices, spiritual issues, all of those kinds of things.

Dr. Jenkins continues, "And I not only have the second education, but I've also attended a monastery and have been licensed to minister. So, I think I'm pretty qualified to handle speaking up and encouraging women to do so. It is my calling, God ordained."

"That sounds great. It sure does sound like you're quite qualified. So, who is this book for?"

"This book is for women of all ages and ethnicity. We have come a long way from being bare foot and pregnant, staying home with our children, cleaning and cooking while serving our mate to working in the workforce and taking positions that are designated for men.

"Being qualified is a tough one, I don't think you have to live a long period of time to be considered "qualified" nor do I feel like my education level qualifies me entirely. I do believe that our phenomenological or lived experience qualifies us to do what we do on purpose.

"I spent more than half of my life being afraid of speaking up and being heard. I remember once when I was a teenager, I was standing outside of a place waiting for my Dad to pick me up. I had on a cute dress with buttons down the back. My Mother always made sure we had the finest clothes. They were probably too expensive, but she wanted us to have what she didn't have when she was growing up. Anyway, an older man came out, and said, 'You can't wait out here, we don't allow that.' In my mind, I was thinking, *Well I just came out of the same door you did and what don't you allow.* I was hurt because I didn't understand. I never said one word. I just moved away from the door and waited for my Dad.

"I have never told anyone that story, until now. Now that I am older, I think he was trying to imply that I was prostituting. He had no reason to say that but, I now know that moment was not about me, but about his perversion.

"I was probably 14 years old, and I looked it. I was dressed appropriately for my age. I chuckle when I think about that now, because today I would have said, exactly what do you mean? I am waiting for my Dad to pick me up. I could think of a few other things I would like to have said, but for now I will choose my words wisely, because that incident was eons ago. The point is that I didn't speak up.

"We were taught to always respect our elders and not talk back. I think those kinds of rules can be taken out of context, because they keep children from talking about things that they need to share with a listening and loving adult. I am not against this practice entirely. I think there needs to be clarification, so that a child understands that they can speak up when something does not feel right. They can ask for help from a parent or a close friend when they are perplexed or indecisive.

"There were many other times I didn't speak up along this journey called life. A few sticks out in my mind like this one. I was asked if I did something. I can't remember what it was, but I did not do it. I was told that I did do it, and I sat there and didn't say a word with tears in my eyes. I held everything inside. It was as though my voice was gone; I remember having a big lump in my throat. I couldn't even get a sound out. I do think these experiences contribute to the behavior of not speaking up and not feeling as though what I had to say was important.

"Yes, I guess I am qualified because I have spent decades trying to hear my own voice, and now I finally can. The fight is still there, I find myself being the last one to be heard in phone conversations and Zoom meetings. Funny how you come to

Speak Up, I Can't Hear You®
The Voice of a Woman

know that you have a distinct sound that has the power to change the lives of others. This is only given by God; I did not arrive at this "purpose" on my own. For 56 years I have experienced this. I take the opportunities presented to share my voice, my vision, my purpose with those around me. I do it intentionally. I also ask questions to open the lines of communication. I ask questions like: 'What's important to you? How do you feel about life? What is your spiritual life like? Do you know how beautiful you are?' I could go on, but I believe questions lead to conversations that open the door to helping others heal along with our own personal healing experience."

To answer your question, I will give an answer that covers women and men of every ethnicity.

"Primarily, this book is for women, all women all over. But you know, today I was encouraged as I posted a question on

Facebook about this particular topic here, and I got some comments from a couple of men who were either fathers raising young girls or men who were concerned about other women in their lives. So, you know, this book is for men too. Maybe there's some men who really want to help women in their lives and they're concerned about some things that have impacted them, their relationships. So, it's for both men and women all over. No specific race, color, or creed. It's for everyone.

"One thing I have learned is that men need a platform to speak up as well. They also need to be heard. I encourage my son to speak up and share what he is thinking not only with me but with those who are blessed to know him and his unique perspective on life."

"Excellent. And who is this book dedicated to?"

Speak Up, I Can't Hear You®
The Voice of a Woman

"I'll have to say, Jim, this book is definitely dedicated to my daughter, Kamara Victoria-Charles Jenkins. And I always say, after her passing, I call her my 'eternal business partner'. She was my business partner before she passed away. And it really helped me orchestrate and facilitate my conferences and get things together. I was laughing as I looked at some notes that she wrote down for me and documented some things as we were planning the conference a few years ago, shortly after her death. And so, I dedicate everything to her in regard to this book.
"She really encouraged me to do this, and I think I owe it to her to complete this task. I hope I can.

"You know I recognize and admire women who can have children without any hinderances. I was 22 years old when I got married and 26 when I had my first child. Nobody knows that during the period between the age 22 and 26 I took fertility treatments, because I couldn't get pregnant. I begged God for my children. When I found out I was pregnant with Kamara (Kami) I was ecstatic about becoming a mother. When it was almost time to have her, I could see her taking breaths rapidly while she was still inside of me.

"I found out she swallowed meconium. I was overdue, and when my water broke my uterus wouldn't dilate. Not to mention that during my pregnancy I fell down a flight of stairs while visiting a church.

"When Kamara was born, she was sick due to swallowing meconium. They called in a specialist, and they explained to me that I might be touching her for the last time.

"Kamara was taken to a children's hospital in Milwaukee, Wisconsin. I was in pain from the c-section procedure, but I went to the hospital every day to see her and touch her. I was confused, hurt, and disappointed. Eventually, she got better and was able to come home. We were so grateful. We watched her grow and deal with her own challenges.

"When Kamara was 13, she had her first seizure. Her life changed from that moment. She wanted so desperately to be healthy. She wanted to be a normal teenager. She wanted to drive and go places without a chaperon. It was hard for the entire family, but most of all it was hard for her. It is still difficult for me to think about what she went through.

"Kamara and I were extremely close. I am close with both of my children. I am like honey to them; they love to be with me and I them.

It was getting close to Christmas in 2018, and Kami complained of hearing her heart beating. I told her let's go to the emergency room and get you checked out.

You've been complaining of this for a few weeks, and nothing has changed. Mind you she was always at the doctor's office for follow-up visits for epilepsy and complications with medications, etc. She didn't want to go but she agreed.

"Well, we went, and we spent the night in the Emergency Department. Kami was gravely ill. She needed a blood transfusion and there was a shortage of blood in the Atlanta metropolitan area. She was weak, she had hemolytic anemia, an autoimmune disease, in which the red blood cells are destroyed faster than they can be made. She wasn't getting the oxygen she needed throughout her body.

"We thought she was coming home. We thought she was going to get better, but she didn't. She went home to be with the Lord on January 3, 2019. I was devastated. She was only 24 years old. She was gone too soon, by my definition. She was a person who loved people and she loved them hard. She needed to be loved. Every night before she went to bed, she would come down the hall and say good night, Mommy, I love you. I still needed her.

"I remember when I was going through tough times in my marriage and Kamara said, "Mommy you are so strong, you don't let people treat you any kind of way. You speak up." That conversation stayed with me even after she transitioned. In that moment, I knew I demonstrated to her what my Mother always said to me, "A woman got to do what a woman got to do." When my mother said this, she meant that we must do whatever it takes to take care of ourselves, our children, and our families. Never let the world get the best of you, trust God."

Mr. Fogle comments and brings us back to the purpose of the book, **"Well, we know you will. And why did you write this book?"**

"I authored this book because initially, let me say this, even back in like 1996 I was an avid *journaler*. So, in journaling and in my prayer time, actually, back when we were using floppy disk, I felt that I heard the Lord saying to me, 'Speak up. I can't hear you.' At the time, I was dealing with growing up and not really being able to speak unless I was spoken to. I could speak, but was anybody really listening?

When you grow up feeling like that, you start to think that what you have to say is not important. You start to think that growing up your opinion doesn't matter. This carried right into adulthood, somehow, I still struggled with really being heard. And so, I had to write this book.

"Honestly, Jim, I had to write this book. I had to finish this because I still sometimes struggle with whether or not I'm speaking up, whether or not I'm the one who just walked in the room and who's going to say what I need to say. I still struggle with that, but now I have a handle on whether or not I can ask myself the question and move forward and make a decision or choose to be that person. Before I was too afraid to speak. So, I think I had to author this book for women all over the world who struggle with this same issue and who needs a push, who needs to know that there's someone to which they can relate."

"Well, that sounds fantastic. Let's get right into your book then. 'Speak Up I Can't Hear You®, The Voice of a Woman.' And let's talk about the chapter entitled, My Voice, My Purpose. So, Dr. Neisa, why is your voice so important?"

SPEAK UP, I CAN'T HEAR YOU®
THE VOICE OF A WOMAN

My Voice, My Purpose

Growing up in a home where you speak when you are spoken to, and you don't get involved in grown folks' conversations can contribute to how much you feel your voice is valued or even heard. Don't get me wrong there were opportunities to share your thoughts, but it was on your level depending upon your age.

For example, what sport do you want to play? What instrument would you like to learn to play? Do you want to join the choir at church? These were the conversations you engaged in. I had so much more to say. I want to be heard. I wanted to ask questions about things that seemed out of reach.

My sister and I shared our thoughts and opinions about things we weren't allowed to engage in growing up. Till this day we laugh about those things and it's funny how she wasn't affected in the same way that I was. The same situation can have a different effect on the people experiencing it.

Henrietta found a way to express herself and she still does. It took years for me to see the value of my voice and to be honest there are still times that I struggle, but I have the tools and resources to push through, to be heard, to share how I feel. When I say tools and resources, I mean I have attended seminars, webinars, and programs in person and virtually centered around communication, speaking, and presenting.

I learned to pray for myself and ask my support circle to pray with me. It's amusing how when you struggle with something you have a vivid memory of the times that caused you the most discomfort.

SPEAK UP, I CAN'T HEAR YOU®
THE VOICE OF A WOMAN

As I mentioned before, I remember being asked if I did something, not sure how old I was but I was young. I knew I didn't do it, but there was no opportunity to even speak. I guess I could have said something, but I was afraid, so I just took the blame. I wanted to scream it wasn't me, I didn't do it, but it was too late. That would have been considered disrespectful. I just walked away bruised by unbelief. I vowed that I would never take away my children's voice.

I must laugh even as I write this because there were times when I almost regretted the level of freedom they operated in as children. I love who they became as individuals who are not afraid to dialogue and share their ideas, their joys and the things that hurt so deeply that took their breath away.

I am amazed at how fearless my son is. One time I made my son so angry that he told me how mad I made him. I could see it in his face, and I just busted out laughing, because I knew it was the verbal freedom that I allow him to tell me he was angry with me and that I should have come to him. I explained to him that I understand that what I did angered him, but I let him know that I am his mom, and I will always protect him. We were fine after that, and we keep the lines of communication open with respect for each other.

My answer to your question is, "A woman's voice is so important because I honestly believe that a woman is at the heart. She's the essence of life. And of course, she's the one who creates life through the process or carries life, shall I say. But I believe that our voice has a distinct sound, and those sounds are different, they vary from one woman to the next. Every woman has something embedded in them that needs to be shared with another woman.

Speak Up, I Can't Hear You®
The Voice of a Woman

I think there's evidence of that sometimes. Maybe while watching Good Morning America, there are a couple of segments on there that show women talking about child rearing or talking about fashion. All of that is a voice speaking topically.

I think it's important that we share it because there's someone who needs to know what you know. We all don't know everything, so there has to be that opportunity and that importance in our voices. No matter again, how big, or how small the topic is, we've got to be able to share that in order to build strength in the female community."

"You have given us something to take with us on Speak Up I Can't Hear You®.

**"Thanks for being on the show and giving us time well spent educating not only women but men also to share what matters most.

"Dr. Jenkins it has been a pleasure and thanks for being on The Jim Fogle Show."

"It has been my pleasure as well. Thanks for having me."

Jim starts speaking directly to the audience, **"Tune in next time. Our next topic will be dressing for success by a highly recommended fashion designer who I will leave nameless until our next show."**

SPEAK UP, I CAN'T HEAR YOU®
THE VOICE OF A WOMAN

It's All Worth Talking About If It Helps Someone Else: Communicating

---

This one is for all my cousin-sisters and cousin-nieces. Let me explain why I call us cousin-sisters and cousin-nieces. We all grew up so close and we all had the same last name in most cases. We are still close till this very day. Sometimes we just call each other to hear the other's voice and say I love you.

We've seen a lot, heard a lot, and learned a whole lot about life and family. Each in our own unique way. We've all had a profound impact on each other, some memories are good and some not so good, but we made it.

I had to write this chapter because we all have a measure of silence that we live by. Let me explain, there are some things that we don't talk about, that's where the pain lives. I found that speaking up about these things when it's necessary can help someone else.

In this case I want to help my cousin-nieces as they move through this thing called life. Our lives are filled with ups and downs and challenges, but I believe they draw us closer to God and make us better people who are more in touch with those around us. We understand things better having been through the good and the not so good.

It was not always easy for me because I was shy. I wanted to be with my mother and that was enough for me when I was younger. As I got older, and I was carrying my first child, it was my father who came to my apartment every day with a Big Mac or whatever my craving was for the day. He drove me to my appointments and just sat with me, by that time I was a daddy's girl.

Growing up there were things said to me by people who I did not really know and sometimes by people I knew, and they knew my parents. They used words to intentionally hurt me.

My homeboy, I call him the circle-historian, said, "If they didn't like yo momma, they don't like you."

Although this is hurtful in some ways, I find it to be true. People would say hurtful things because they didn't like my mother. Yes, she was outspoken, and she did not play. If you came for her, you better be ready for the trajectory of her words. They could cut like a knife and in the expression on her face you knew she was not playing by any means.

Our friends that we grew up with used to say, "Ms. Ivy don't play."

Having a strict mother made me respect the rules and guidelines that came with life. She wanted more for her children and her family. She taught us that hard work pays off. Do your job and do it well. You can be the best at what you do.

Disciplining your children is necessary and there are various ways to do it. Now I must admit that when I had my children, I didn't want to spank them. It would break my heart if I thought I would have to discipline them. My mother would laugh and tell me, "They gone whip your behind and leave you sitting at that pond behind your house."

When my children started getting older speaking up could be tough, but by then they were used to telling me how they felt. I didn't want to raise them under the guise of only speaking when they were spoken to or not engaging in discussion with grown folk.

Speak Up, I Can't Hear You®
The Voice of a Woman

Honestly, my sister engaged even when she was told not to, even if she was only listening. I think this made her more aware, and more in tune with the ways of life. She is much wittier than I am. She sees things differently because of that exposure. Oftentimes, she "schools" me on what's going on.

I want my cousin-sisters to know that we all did good. We are who we are, created in the image of God. We all love God deeply, we cook, clean, raise our children, run our own businesses, go to church, shop, love, laugh, and live our lives to the best of our abilities. Our common denominator is family. We love each other and we recognize the silence and pain that shows up when you least expect it. When we get together, we can just start talking and the next thing you know we are crying and then the healing comes. It's a beautiful thing to witness.

I remember when Kami died, and all my family came from near and far. We shared our collective moments, but we had some individual moments too. Those were the moments that I gathered strength and determination. I was so broken, I didn't know who I was without her, but I found strength in the love that was shown. My words can't fully capture the essence of that time in my life; I struggle to find the right words to describe that period of my life. Spiritually I was being strengthened by our coming together.

I just want my cousin-sisters and cousin-nieces to know that we need family, no matter what was said in the past. We really don't have all the details of someone else's situation. We need each other. Family dynamics are funny how we live, love, fight, fall out and fall back in again. It's just the way it goes, but what I am saying to you is never let it fall out without getting back together again.

SPEAK UP, I CAN'T HEAR YOU®
THE VOICE OF A WOMAN

On another note, we have all had our experiences with men. Some of us are married, were married, and some of us are single. I can say for myself I have had my experiences, when I was married and single and when it was good it was good, but when it wasn't, it just wasn't.

I am not ashamed of the hardships I've experienced or the marvelous times I shared with someone that I love with everything within me. Love is a beautiful thing. God is love and he is patient, kind, and forgiving. True love does not come with abusive words or actions. It doesn't make you feel like you are less than. When you find someone who loves you for who you are, love hard without regret.

I want you all to know that it hasn't been easy, with God all things are possible. Life has been filled with ups and downs good and bad, but I have come this far by faith and by having a good support system. Someone that God allows to be close enough to me that I can share my deepest thoughts and experiences with, knowing that they won't judge me, but they will offer me good sound advice after they have prayed for guidance and words to say.

It's so important to communicate. Many relationships have ended because of a lack of communication. We communicate in so many ways, verbally and nonverbally. We must express what we feel so that we don't create expectations for others that they have no ideal about. Say what you feel, choose your words wisely.

Share your deepest thoughts with God and He will bring the resources you need to help others. Don't be ashamed or afraid to talk to God. He already knows, He just wants us to come to Him so that He can help us.

I want you to understand that our flaws are powerful. Know that God will give you beauty for ashes. I am a witness to this.

SPEAK UP, I CAN'T HEAR YOU®
THE VOICE OF A WOMAN

Love yourself, completely, so that you can fully love others.

The Voice Of A Woman

A woman's voice has the innate ability to save the world. Her voice is full of compassion, sympathy, and empathy for the entire universe. A woman's voice along with her many attributes shapes and molds the future of her children, siblings, cousins, friends, sisters, and communities. Her voice encourages and speaks peace to her brother, husband, neighbors, family, and colleagues. A woman's voice is Global!!!

If pushed, her voice can crush and move mountains that couldn't be moved for centuries "… to uproot and tear down, to destroy and overthrow, to build and to plant." Jeremiah 1:10 (NIV)

Although Jeremiah is a male figure used in this text, I want to express a point. Jeremiah was afraid to speak to the people.

He was young. God told him not to look at the faces. What he had to say was within him. The words were like fire in his bones waiting to be released. It does not matter how young we are or areas where we think we lack. Our voice must be heard.

Make no mistake there are some things that must be overthrown in a woman's life. Such as:

- negativity,
- self-doubt,
- resentment,
- anger,
- disappointment,
- self-hate,
- self-inflicted pain,
- double mindedness,
- low self-esteem,
- depression,
- oppression,
- sorrow,

Speak Up, I Can't Hear You®
The Voice of a Woman

- disappointment,
- loneliness,
- self-pity,
- rejection,
- fear of love, and
- just to name a few.

But these are things we go through daily.

My bible tells me in Jeremiah 29:11 "That the Lord declares, I know the plans that I have towards you, plans to prosper you and not to harm you, plans to give you hope and a future." [Paraphrasing]

Her voice speaks of faith, hope, and love for those who have never been loved or touched.

Love is patient, love is kind. It does not envy, it does not boast, it is not proud. It does not dishonor others, it is not self-seeking, it is not easily angered, it keeps no record of wrongs. Love does not delight in evil but rejoices with the truth. It always protects, always trusts, always hopes, always perseveres. (I Cor. 13:4-7 - NIV)

Ah, a woman's voice is powerful it reeks of innovation (means to add something new) and promises of a future that can heal a nation. Her voice empowers, equips, and encourages even the most far away stranger.

"The tongue has the power of life and death, and those who love it will eat its fruit." (Proverbs18:21- NIV)

A woman's voice can speak her own future, prosperity, opportunities, and businesses into existence. Her voice has the aptitude to change the unchangeable. A woman's voice has the accomplishment to forgive even the most horrific occurrence that can impact an entire generation. Her voice is resilient; able to stand the test of time, bounce back, recover, press past the pain (my 3 P's), and move forward.

Speak Up, I Can't Hear You®
The Voice of a Woman

What are you using your voice to speak! You choose what you are going to say! Our voice can reach back and change a generation in the future.

Look around the room and see and hear the voices of the women around you in the room today. Look at your sister and say - my voice, my vision, my dream, my purpose. Make it a reality. Call those things that be not as though they were. It's only by faith.

"In the same way, faith by itself, if it is not accompanied by action, is dead." (James 2:17 - NIV).

Now faith is the substance of things hoped for, the evidence of things not seen (Hebrews 11:1 - KJV).

Always Infuse Love When You Speak

Love is a complex emotion.

Love can appear in heartfelt connections, companionships, and expressive communications that demonstrate our feelings.

Love is a crucial part of the human experience. When love is infused in our conversation it takes what we say to a whole different vibe. The power of love is amazing. When we give love and it is reciprocated, it makes us feel loved. When it is not, we might decide not to give or show love. It is our decision to make. Nonetheless, it is healthy for us to give and show love towards others even when others do not know how to love.

In I Corinthians 13:1 it says, "If I speak in the tongues of men or of angels, but do not have love, I am only a resounding gong or a clanging cymbal." (NIV) Therefore, when we speak, we must do it in love.

As I take this early morning flight to Chicago. I ask myself why I always have a need to go back to Chicagoland. I answer that question without hesitation. It comes to mind like an old Donny Hathaway treasure, "A Song for You" the live show at The Troubadour, Los Angeles version.

Whenever I listen to this song and I hear Mr. Hathaway say, "Baby can't you see through me, so we are alone now, and I am singing this song to you. You taught me precious secrets of a true love withholding nothing. You came out in front when I was hiding. Hey, hey, but now I am so much better." No other musical genius sings of love the way Mr. Hathaway does. His passion, his phenomenological experience heralds from the words of his lyrics.

Speak Up, I Can't Hear You®
The Voice of a Woman

Chicagoland is where I learned "love begins at home." I come back to my beginnings for restoration, healing, and love. All of these benefits are equal to good mental and physical health. Love makes us happy, relieves stress, and eases anxiety. It helps us take care of ourselves better, including living longer.

We need love to have a balanced life. It is also important to release love toward others.

There can't be restoration without love, and there can't be healing without restoration, so on and so forth. They depend on each other. "Above all, have fervent unfailing love for one another, because love covers a multitude of sin [it overlooks unkindness and unselfishly seeks the best for others]." (I Peter 4:8 - AMP)

Getting the opportunity to visit the church where I first felt the love of God. Yes, that feeling is unforgettable, so I go back as often as I can, and I always will. My family is also there and whether they know it or not, they give me love, they strengthen me. The more I give it the more I get. Reciprocity makes such good sense. So, what am I saying, don't hide love. It should be present and upfront, exuding from you.

I had a conversation with a friend the other day. Y'all he is wisdom personified, let's just call him "T". He explained the power of his voice allows him the opportunity to express his innermost feelings. He explained that when he is loud and stern in his message delivery that is just his voice expressing his level of passion. He's not angry, what he is trying to relay in his message is important and it can't be expressed at a low volume because it won't have the same effect. I so enjoy our conversations because I always learn something.

The older I get the more I look for the love of God everywhere and in everyone. I believe His love is there we just must take the opportunity to look without judgment, just love.

When we speak, we must speak with love, because our words have power. So much so that we can change the trajectory of someone's life by our word choice. We are more powerful than we know. We must always try to choose our words wisely. I pray that we will love each other more. I think 12-time grammy nominated, Dianna Ross said it best when she sang, "What the world needs now is love sweet love, that's the only thing that there is just too little of."

MY VOICE

My voice speaks volumes whenever I speak. This is why I put careful thought into what I am saying. I have created the world around me with the words that I have spoken.

When my life is going in the opposite direction of what I am expecting, I speak the world around me that I want to see. Eventually, it manifests itself at times when I least expect it.

My voice is a powerful tool that can convey a lot of information beyond the words I speak.

My voice reveals a lot about who I am. My voice can also reveal my emotions and mental state. For instance, when I am happy, my voice tends to be more upbeat and energetic. On the other hand, when I am sad or upset, my voice may become quieter or more subdued. Similarly, when I am nervous or anxious, my voice may become shaky or strained.

Overall, my voice is an important tool for communication that can reveal a lot about who I am. By paying attention to how I speak and how others speak to me, I can gain valuable insights into who I am and who others are.

My voice speaks that I can be anything I want to be.

My voice says I can be who I am created to be.

My voice says that prayer refocused my mind on the power of prayer and not the pettiness of people (TDJ).

My voice says that I am healed, whole, transformed by the renewing of my mind.

Speak Up, I Can't Hear You®
The Voice of a Woman

My voice says that I am complete, fearfully, and wonderfully made.

My voice confirms that I am God inspired, validated, sealed, saved to the uttermost, established, positioned, and blessed.

SPEAK UP, I CAN'T HEAR YOU!!!

This phrase speaks things into existence.

Speak Up I Can't Hear You!

Speak Up! Why Can't I Hear You?

BIOGRAPHY

Dr. Neisa R. Jenkins, RHIA, FAHIMA, is the founder of I Am Beautiful Too Ministry. She is the mother of Kamara Victoria-Charles Jenkins and Charles Isaiah-Fitzgerald Jenkins.

She is also a full professor in the College of Health Sciences at a University in the Midwest.

Jenkins earned her Bachelor of Science degree in Health Information Management at the University of Illinois (Chicago), a Master of Arts in Health Information Management at the College of St. Scholastica, and her Doctor of Education at Walden University.

Jenkins entered the study of Family Priest Intercession through the Inner Court Prayer Ministry under the teaching of Minister Anita Rollins and Apostle Dr. Pernell H. Hewing founder and President of Share-A-Prayer and Word Theological School of Ministry of Whitewater, Wisconsin.

During this time of study, prayer, fasting, and consecration unto the Lord, she acknowledged the assignment from God to worship Him in spirit and truth, being a vessel fortified in the Word of God.

Dr. Jenkins is a woman of God who has been appointed and anointed by God. She has a passion to help women reach their full potential and purpose.

Dr. Jenkins' hope is to create platforms where the "Voice Of A Woman" can be heard, and her dreams, visions, and aspirations can be manifested all over the world.

Speak Up, I Can't Hear You®
The Voice of a Woman

On the next several pages you have the opportunity to journal and explore your personal thoughts, emotions, and experiences. These pages provide a private space for you to start the healing process by clarifying your thoughts, identifying personal challenges and triumphs in your lived experiences.

This is your opportunity to create a record of your personal growth, development, and flaws. Nurture yourself, set goals and celebrate, "You".

In a few months revisit these pages and see how far you have come. Use this as a time of self-discovery and establish a deeper connection within yourself.

There are a couple blank pages that I hope you will use to write your own story, "Speak Up, I Can't Hear You."

SPEAK UP, I CAN'T HEAR YOU®
THE VOICE OF A WOMAN

JOURNAL

Write about what is important to you that you would like others to know:

_____
_____
_____
_____
_____
_____
_____
_____
_____
_____
_____
_____
_____
_____
_____
_____
_____
_____

Speak Up, I Can't Hear You®
The Voice of a Woman

Speak Up, I Can't Hear You®
The Voice of a Woman

Write what you would like to speak about in a forum with other women:

_____
_____
_____
_____
_____
_____
_____
_____
_____
_____
_____
_____
_____
_____
_____
_____
_____
_____
_____
_____
_____
_____
_____
_____
_____
_____

Speak Up, I Can't Hear You®
The Voice of a Woman

Speak Up, I Can't Hear You®

The Voice of a Woman

Since it is vital to your expansion, what would you like to share with others that will benefit everyone:

_____
_____
_____
_____
_____
_____
_____
_____
_____
_____
_____
_____
_____
_____
_____
_____
_____
_____
_____
_____
_____
_____
_____
_____

Speak Up, I Can't Hear You®

The Voice of a Woman

_____
_____
_____
_____
_____
_____
_____
_____
_____
_____
_____
_____
_____
_____
_____
_____
_____
_____
_____
_____
_____
_____
_____
_____
_____

Speak Up, I Can't Hear You®
The Voice of a Woman

What are some of the topics you would like to research and speak about?

SPEAK UP, I CAN'T HEAR YOU®
THE VOICE OF A WOMAN

Speak Up, I Can't Hear You®
The Voice of a Woman

What are some of the encouraging words you would like to say to yourself?

_____
_____
_____
_____
_____
_____
_____
_____
_____
_____
_____
_____
_____
_____
_____
_____
_____
_____
_____
_____
_____
_____
_____

Speak Up, I Can't Hear You®
The Voice of a Woman

_____
_____
_____
_____
_____
_____
_____
_____
_____
_____
_____
_____
_____
_____
_____
_____
_____
_____
_____
_____
_____
_____
_____
_____

Speak Up, I Can't Hear You®
The Voice of a Woman

Where do you believe your words can take you?

_____
_____
_____
_____
_____
_____
_____
_____
_____
_____
_____
_____
_____
_____
_____
_____
_____
_____
_____
_____
_____
_____
_____
_____
_____

Speak Up, I Can't Hear You®
The Voice of a Woman

Speak Up, I Can't Hear You®

The Voice of a Woman

Write what you wanted to say when you were younger that you were afraid to say:

_____
_____
_____
_____
_____
_____
_____
_____
_____
_____
_____
_____
_____
_____
_____
_____
_____
_____
_____
_____
_____
_____
_____
_____
_____

Speak Up, I Can't Hear You®
The Voice of a Woman

SPEAK UP, I CAN'T HEAR YOU®
THE VOICE OF A WOMAN

While in a meeting with others, write what you felt was most important to you and what you would have added to the discussion:

_____
_____
_____
_____
_____
_____
_____
_____
_____
_____
_____
_____
_____
_____
_____
_____
_____
_____
_____
_____
_____
_____

Speak Up, I Can't Hear You®
The Voice of a Woman

_____
_____
_____
_____
_____
_____
_____
_____
_____
_____
_____
_____
_____
_____
_____
_____
_____
_____
_____
_____
_____
_____

SPEAK UP, I CAN'T HEAR YOU®
THE VOICE OF A WOMAN

Give yourself permission to express yourself with words that are edifying:

_____
_____
_____
_____
_____
_____
_____
_____
_____
_____
_____
_____
_____
_____
_____
_____
_____
_____
_____
_____
_____
_____
_____
_____

Speak Up, I Can't Hear You®
The Voice of a Woman

Speak Up, I Can't Hear You®
The Voice of a Woman

When doubt comes to mind, speak words that would counterattack the negativity then write them down:

_____
_____
_____
_____
_____
_____
_____
_____
_____
_____
_____
_____
_____
_____
_____
_____
_____
_____
_____
_____
_____
_____

Speak Up, I Can't Hear You®
The Voice of a Woman

Speak Up, I Can't Hear You®
The Voice of a Woman

Was there something that happened in your past when you think about it today you would have handled it differently? If so, write about what you would change:

Speak Up, I Can't Hear You®
The Voice of a Woman

_____
_____
_____
_____
_____
_____
_____
_____
_____
_____
_____
_____
_____
_____
_____
_____
_____
_____
_____
_____
_____
_____
_____

Speak Up, I Can't Hear You®
The Voice of a Woman

Write about how you demonstrated the authentic you today:

Speak Up, I Can't Hear You®
The Voice of a Woman

Speak Up, I Can't Hear You®
The Voice of a Woman

Describe what it feels like when you are at your best:

Speak Up, I Can't Hear You®
The Voice of a Woman

Speak Up, I Can't Hear You®
The Voice of a Woman

Where did you put your energy today? Was the outcome positive:

_____
_____
_____
_____
_____
_____
_____
_____
_____
_____
_____
_____
_____
_____
_____
_____
_____
_____
_____
_____
_____
_____
_____

Speak Up, I Can't Hear You®
The Voice of a Woman

Speak Up, I Can't Hear You®
The Voice of a Woman

Describe a past hurt that still has some residue in your heart, how will you seek complete healing?

_____
_____
_____
_____
_____
_____
_____
_____
_____
_____
_____
_____
_____
_____
_____
_____
_____
_____
_____
_____
_____
_____

Speak Up, I Can't Hear You®
The Voice of a Woman

Speak Up, I Can't Hear You®
The Voice of a Woman

Write about a moment when you spoke up in love and it was received with love. Describe how it feels:

_____
_____
_____
_____
_____
_____
_____
_____
_____
_____
_____
_____
_____
_____
_____
_____
_____
_____
_____
_____
_____
_____
_____

Speak Up, I Can't Hear You®
The Voice of a Woman

Speak Up, I Can't Hear You®
The Voice of a Woman

How do you want to use your voice to impact the world?

Speak Up, I Can't Hear You®
The Voice of a Woman

Speak Up, I Can't Hear You®
The Voice of a Woman

How will you use your inner voice to heal others?

Speak Up, I Can't Hear You®
The Voice of a Woman

Speak Up, I Can't Hear You®
The Voice of a Woman

Describe a way that you will commit to being your sister's keeper:

Speak Up, I Can't Hear You®
The Voice of a Woman

SPEAK UP, I CAN'T HEAR YOU®
THE VOICE OF A WOMAN

What awakens your passion deep down inside?

_____
_____
_____
_____
_____
_____
_____
_____
_____
_____
_____
_____
_____
_____
_____
_____
_____
_____
_____
_____
_____
_____

Speak Up, I Can't Hear You®
The Voice of a Woman

_____
_____
_____
_____
_____
_____
_____
_____
_____
_____
_____
_____
_____
_____
_____
_____
_____
_____
_____
_____
_____
_____
_____
_____
_____

Speak Up, I Can't Hear You®
The Voice of a Woman

How will you ascend to the next level?

Speak Up, I Can't Hear You®
The Voice of a Woman

_____
_____
_____
_____
_____
_____
_____
_____
_____
_____
_____
_____
_____
_____
_____
_____
_____
_____
_____
_____
_____
_____
_____
_____

Speak Up, I Can't Hear You®
The Voice of a Woman

Take a moment to breathe, describe what this feels like to you:

_____
_____
_____
_____
_____
_____
_____
_____
_____
_____
_____
_____
_____
_____
_____
_____
_____
_____
_____
_____
_____
_____
_____
_____
_____

Speak Up, I Can't Hear You®
The Voice of a Woman

Speak Up, I Can't Hear You®
The Voice of a Woman

Describe a nostalgic feeling that causes you to reset:

_____
_____
_____
_____
_____
_____
_____
_____
_____
_____
_____
_____
_____
_____
_____
_____
_____
_____
_____
_____
_____
_____
_____
_____

Speak Up, I Can't Hear You®
The Voice of a Woman

Speak Up, I Can't Hear You®
The Voice of a Woman

Ask yourself, "How can I help?" Describe the steps you will take to begin helping:

Speak Up, I Can't Hear You®
The Voice of a Woman

_____
_____
_____
_____
_____
_____
_____
_____
_____
_____
_____
_____
_____
_____
_____
_____
_____
_____
_____
_____
_____
_____
_____

Speak Up, I Can't Hear You®
The Voice of a Woman

Describe what "God's Grace" looks like in your life:

_____
_____
_____
_____
_____
_____
_____
_____
_____
_____
_____
_____
_____
_____
_____
_____
_____
_____
_____
_____
_____
_____

Speak Up, I Can't Hear You®
The Voice of a Woman

Speak Up, I Can't Hear You®
The Voice of a Woman

Take a moment to look at the sky. What's the first thing that comes to mind?

Speak Up, I Can't Hear You®
The Voice of a Woman

Speak Up, I Can't Hear You®
The Voice of a Woman

How have you extended grace to others today?

Speak Up, I Can't Hear You®
The Voice of a Woman

SPEAK UP, I CAN'T HEAR YOU®
THE VOICE OF A WOMAN

Describe what's next for you:

_____
_____
_____
_____
_____
_____
_____
_____
_____
_____
_____
_____
_____
_____
_____
_____
_____
_____
_____
_____
_____
_____
_____
_____
_____

Speak Up, I Can't Hear You®
The Voice of a Woman

Speak Up, I Can't Hear You®
The Voice of a Woman

How will you give back today and, in the days to come?

Speak Up, I Can't Hear You®
The Voice of a Woman

Speak Up, I Can't Hear You®
The Voice of a Woman

What was your positive affirmation for today?

Speak Up, I Can't Hear You®
The Voice of a Woman

Speak Up, I Can't Hear You®
The Voice of a Woman

Explain ways that you showed self-compassion and self-love:

_____
_____
_____
_____
_____
_____
_____
_____
_____
_____
_____
_____
_____
_____
_____
_____
_____
_____
_____
_____
_____
_____
_____
_____

Speak Up, I Can't Hear You®
The Voice of a Woman

Speak Up, I Can't Hear You®
The Voice of a Woman

Think about your inner circle. Who are your positive influencers and how do they influence you?

_____
_____
_____
_____
_____
_____
_____
_____
_____
_____
_____
_____
_____
_____
_____
_____
_____
_____
_____
_____
_____
_____
_____

Speak Up, I Can't Hear You®
The Voice of a Woman

Speak Up, I Can't Hear You®
The Voice of a Woman

When is the last time you celebrated, YOU? Write down five (5) of your celebrated successes:

_____
_____
_____
_____
_____
_____
_____
_____
_____
_____
_____
_____
_____
_____
_____
_____
_____
_____
_____
_____
_____
_____
_____
_____

Speak Up, I Can't Hear You®
The Voice of a Woman

Speak Up, I Can't Hear You®
The Voice of a Woman

Start Writing Your Own Story

_____
_____
_____
_____
_____
_____
_____
_____
_____
_____
_____
_____
_____
_____
_____
_____
_____
_____
_____
_____
_____
_____
_____
_____
_____

SPEAK UP, I CAN'T HEAR YOU®
THE VOICE OF A WOMAN

www.ingramcontent.com/pod-product-compliance
Lightning Source LLC
LaVergne TN
LVHW061550070526
838199LV00077B/6979